Speed Up Your Computer

Computer

A Non Techie, Easy to Implement, Step By Step Guide On How to Defrag and Clean Up Your Computer

By: Todd Black

ISBN-13: 978-1481944861

PUBLISHED BY:
IMT, LLC

DISCLAIMER AND TERMS OF USE

No information contained in this book should be considered as physical, health related, financial, tax, or legal advice. Your reliance upon information and content obtained by you at or through this publication is solely at your own risk. The author assumes no liability or responsibly for damage or injury to you, other persons, or property arising from any use of any product, information, idea, or instruction contained in the content provided to you through this book.

Clear up clutter on your PC

Thank you for your purchase. Within the next few pages, one will discover an easy, step by step instruction manual that will show screen shots on how to defragment, and erase unnecessary files from your computer. Your computer can have a twofold benefit by performing the actions outlined in this book. First, it should help your PC run faster. Secondly, it should clear up disk space on your PC, which means your computer should run faster and more proficiently.

All actions performed on your PC on a daily basis can use a small percentage of your computers disk space. Downloading, surfing the web, creating files, or opening a page are all tasks that take up valuable disk space.

Most people do not ever know they need to clean

up these files on their computer. These files are no longer needed but remain until they are erased. The actions one performs on a daily, weekly, and monthly basis clutter up your hard drive over time and clogs up your computer. This clutter can cause your computers speed to slow down and eat up valuable disk space.

The goal with this guide is to keep your computer's disk space compressed and clean up your computer so it can perform at its optimum speed, providing the user with the best experience.

First let's find out how much space remains on your computer. Second, we are going to increase this space allowing your computer to work more efficiently. Third, we are going to defragment your computer, which will remove unwanted files from your hard drive. It is like having tiny holes on your hard drive. Defragmenting your hard drive will compress these holes giving more space on the hard drive.

Your computer only has a certain amount of space. These measurements consist of kilobytes, megabytes, or gigabytes, which represent how much space a file takes up on your computer.

The smallest measurement of space starts with kilobytes, then increases to megabytes, and then increases to gigabytes. So to understand how much space remains, we must learn how many kilobytes equal a megabyte and again how many megabytes equal a gigabyte.

Knowing these basic measurements help to determine the space that remains when looking at your files on your computer. Let's look at the simple measurements.

Disk Space:

1000 kilobytes = 1 megabyte

1000 megabytes = 1 gigabyte

Each level increases or decreases by 1000 to get to the next level of measurement.

Simply follow the example I'll provide and go to a property on your computer. I am going to use my "Image" folder.

Right click on the folder:

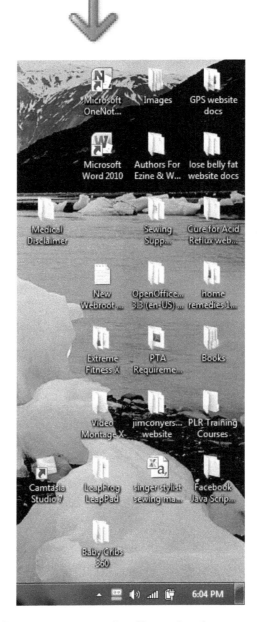

Next, click on "Properties" at the bottom of the

drop down screen. The properties show this folder

takes up 6.22 MB (6,527,974 bytes).

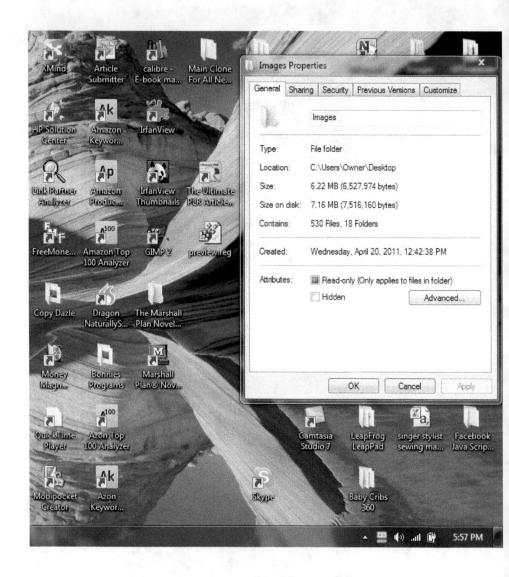

The "Images" folder is taking up 6.22 MB's. This folder is 6220 kilobytes. The images folder will provide one a reference to see if a file is large or small. Use this easy process with any of your files, pictures, EBook's, videos or program files to see how large they are.

Next, we will be finding out how much space is on your computer.

Locate the start button in the lower left hand corner of your screen. Click on the "Start" button.

Next, click on "Computer."

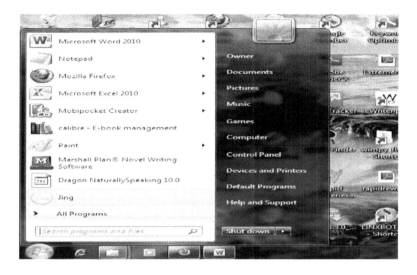

Here is an image of "Computer" opened.

We will be concerning ourselves with the Local Disk (C:) drive.

Next, we are going to right click on the Local (C:) drive. A window will open up. Scroll down to the bottom of the window and click on "Properties".

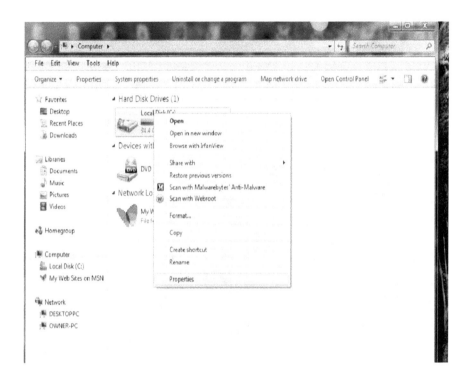

A new window will open displaying how much free space and used space are on your computer.

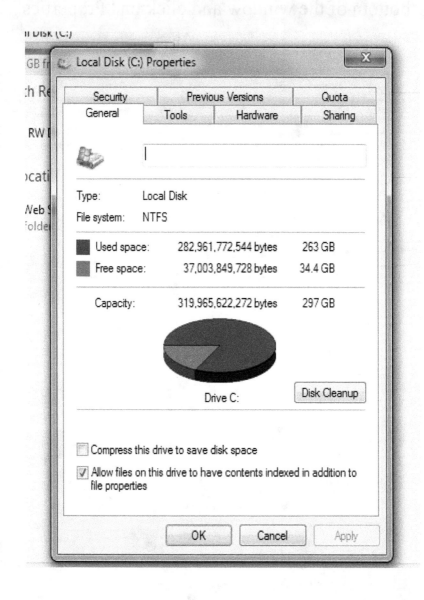

The pink color of the pie chart displays the free space on my computer. It shows my computer has 34.4 GB of free space on my PC. It also shows in the blue section of the pie chart, that my used space is 263 GB.

Your computers Capacity can be found just above the pie chart. My computer shows it has a capacity of 297 GB.

My computer is using 263 GB of space out of the 297 GB's my computer offers. My computer is remarkably full and is probably running slower than it should be.

We are now ready to clean up the PC. Next, click
on the "Disk Cleanup" button just to the lower
right of the pie chart.

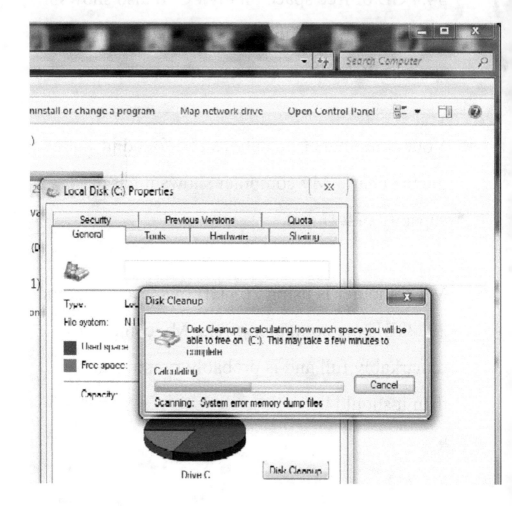

Your computer is now calculating how much space it will be able to free up on your (C:) drive. It usually takes only a few minutes.

Once your computer has finished computing the information it will bring up a new screen.

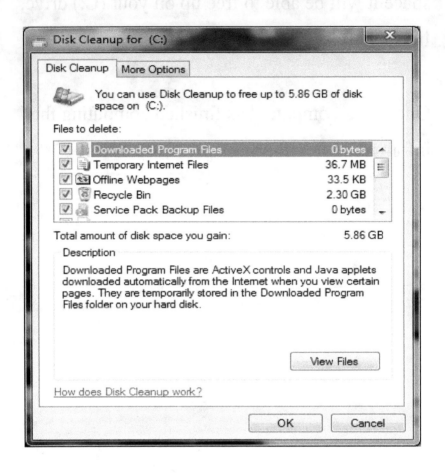

The above screen shot is projecting 5.86 GB of space to be retrieved once you continue. Make sure to view the checked boxes before continuing to verify you want to remove those specific files before continuing.

Before deleting any files, verify the suggested checked boxes are the correct files to be deleted. Once one verifies these are the correct files to be deleted, simply click the "OK" button to begin the process.

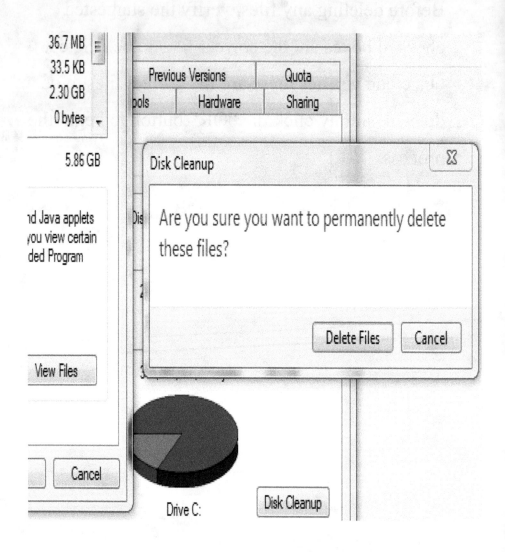

It will now ask to confirm the selected files are the correct files to delete before starting the deletion process. Once verified, simply click on "Delete Files".

Your computer will start to complete the deletion of the selected files.

It can take your computer up to or more than 20 minutes to complete this process.

Speed Up My Computer

Once your computer finishes the operation then click the "apply" button in the lower right hand corner of the dialog box. The process can take several hours to complete. Once complete the computer should have created more space for your hard drive.

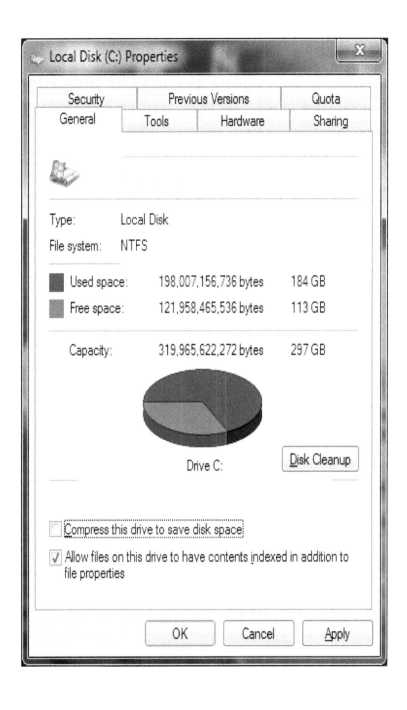

Now that, we have created more space on your hard drive, we need to defragment the computer which will compress the holes together creating more space.

Next, let's go back to the following screen and click on "tools".

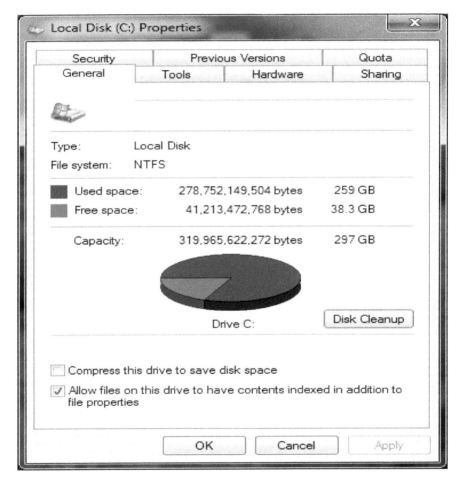

A popup window will appear that looks like the image below.

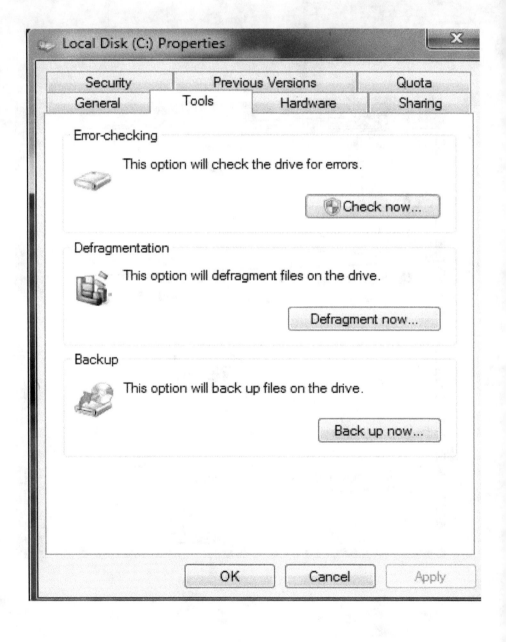

Now, come down to the middle option "Defragmentation". Click on the "Defragment now" button.

Click the "Defragment now" button and the following screen like the image below will appear.

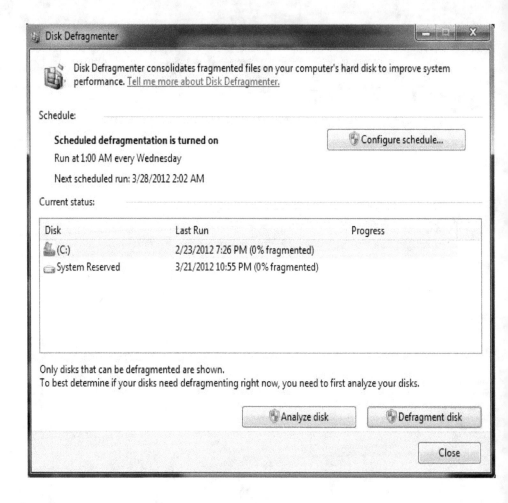

Then click on the "Analyze Disk" button.

Todd Black

Your computer will go to work and determine if your disk needs to be defragmented.

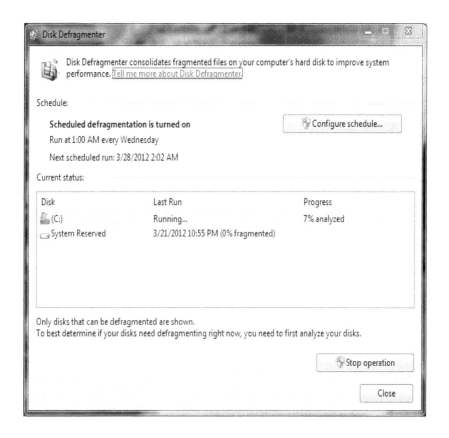

My computer screen displays the (C:) drive that is highlighted and is running. The progress was at 7% analyzed.

Speed Up My Computer

My computer provided an analysis showing it did not need to be defragmented. Under the highlighted (C:) drive, the date and time then (0% fragmented) displayed. Just above that, I run the disk defragmenter on a schedule, which I set to run at 6:00 a.m. one day a month.

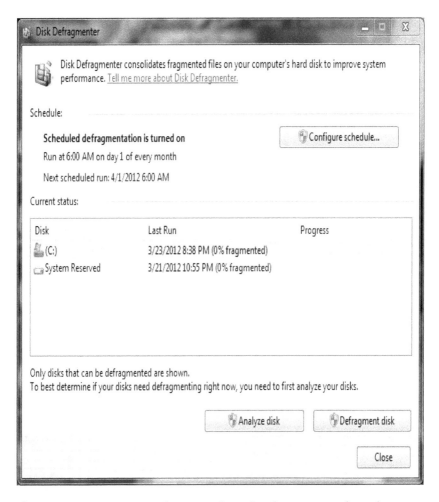

If your computer shows that it does need to be defragmented, simply click the "Defragment Disk" button. Your computer will start compressing and defragmenting the files on your hard drive.

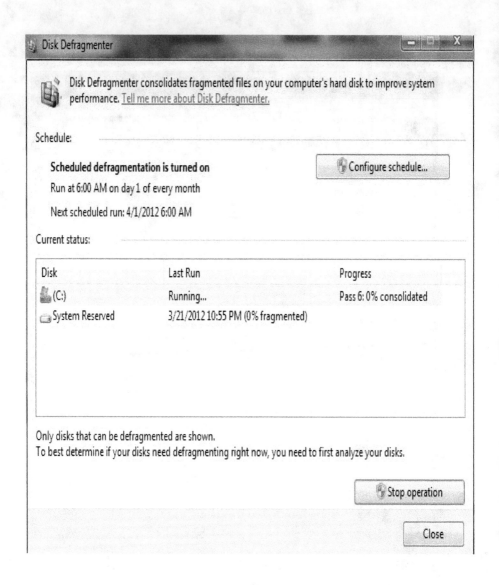

I would suggest running the Defragmenting component at night before retiring for the evening. The process can take a couple of hours to complete.

Cleaning up your computer is as easy as that. I would recommend performing the above steps every couple of months to keep your computer running at its optimum condition.

One's computer can become cluttered and slow down performance without proper maintenance. Implementing the easy steps outlined in this book can provide a vast improvement in its performance.

How to Protect Your PC from Malware, Spyware and other Threats to Your Computer

Malware and Spyware are programs that your computer may pick up from time to time by surfing the net.

These programs run in the background on your PC, which track your actions and the sites your computer visit. These programs then collect data to use for marketing purchases and statistics.

These programs can bog down your PC by using too many of your computers resources. A simple solution to this problem is to install an Anti-Malware program. Anti-Malware can locate other threats such as Spyware, and can detect these programs, quarantine them so they can easily be removed from your computer.

There are many different Anti-Malware software's to choose from, but I use and recommend using free Anti-Malware software called Malwarebytes. Go to www.malwarebytes.org/free and download a free copy of this awesome software.

Simply scroll to the bottom of the page and click the "Free Download" button to install the free version. The free version is what I use.

You will now be brought to the free sign up page.

Malwarebytes Free Download

Please fill out the form below to register for your free product. The download will be delivered via e-mail.

E-Mail:

First:

Last:

☑ Sign up for our monthly email regarding special offers, newsletters and product updates. You can unsubscribe at any time from these mails.

Register

Note: As a security company, we are committed to keeping your privacy safe. Your e-mail address will not be sold or shared.

© 2011 Malwarebytes Corporation   Home | Privacy Policy

Simply fill in your relevant details and click "Register". Malwarebytes offers an option to sign up for their monthly email newsletter.

Next, a thank you screen should appear to advise you to check the email you provided in the download.

Malwarebytes Free Download

Thank you! Please check your e-mail for your download of Malwarebytes Anti-Malware FREE.

® 2011 Malwarebytes Corporation   Home | Privacy Policy

Go to the email Inbox that was selected and locate a message that is something like the one below.

Thank you for registering for your Malwarebytes product.

Run our Free scan to find and remove Malware that many well-known antivirus applications fail to detect. By downloading our free version you agree to sign up for a monthly email regarding special offers, newsletters and product updates. You can unsubscribe at any time from these mails.

Click the button below to download our Free Version:

Our full PRO version does much more than just Detect and Remove! Protect your PC from ever getting infected with Malware. Don't risk losing your personal data to criminals.

For just $24.95 consumers get a lifetime license including Real-time Active Malware Protection and Malicious Website Blocking.

- Over 5.0 Billion Pieces of Malware removed
- Compatible with Leading Antivirus software
- Free Customer Support

Simply click the blue "Download Free Version" button to download your program onto your computer.

The Malwarebytes download page should appear.

Malwarebytes Free Download

Thank you for confirming your e-mail address. Look forward to future emails from Malwarebytes providing special promotions, newletters, and product updates. Your information will not be sold or shared.

Please click the link below to download your Malwarebytes product.

Malwarebytes Anti-Malware

If malware is detected, we highly advise purchasing the PRO Version, because your current Anti-Virus is not protecting your PC.
Purchase the Full Version of Malwarebytes.

Questions or Suggestions?

Website: http://helpdesk.malwarebytes.org
E-mail: support@malwarebytes.org

©2011 Malwarebytes Corporation   Home | Privacy Policy

Next, click the blue hyperlink that states: "Malwarebytes Anti-Malware to start your download".

Next, a Malwarebytes set up window should appear. Click the "Save File" button.

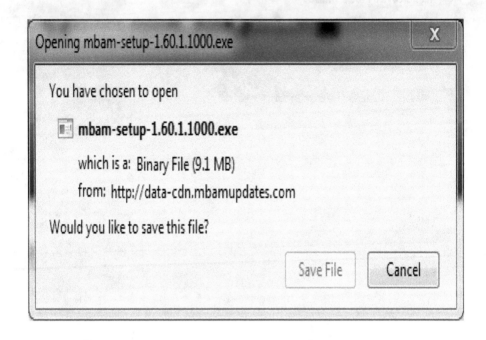

The "download" program window should appear. Left click the .exe File twice, quickly. The file will open.

Next, click the "Run" button to start the download process.

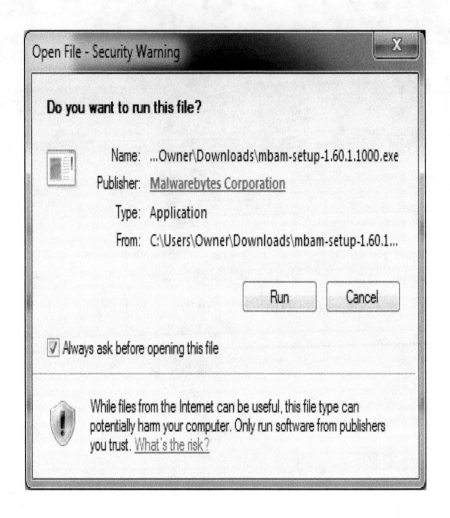

Todd Black

Next, the Malwarebytes setup Wizard should
appear. Use the setup Wizard to install the
program on your computer.

Next, click the "Next" button. The license
agreement should appear. It is particularly
important to read and agree to the terms before
proceeding. If the terms are acceptable, tick the "I
accept the agreement" button to proceed.,

The important information screen should appear.

After reading and agreeing to the software terms, click the "Next" button to continue.

The destination screen, showing where the program is going to be installed should appear. Their recommended default setting is usually the best setting. If this is acceptable, click "Next".

The following screen will advise where the setup files will be downloaded. Again the default setting is usually best. To agree, click the "Next" button.

Next, a desktop icon screen should appear with the box next to it ticked. Creating a desktop icon will make it easier to locate the program when it is time to run it again. To create the shortcut icon, click the "Next" button to continue.

Next, the ready to install screen should appear.

Click the "Install" button.

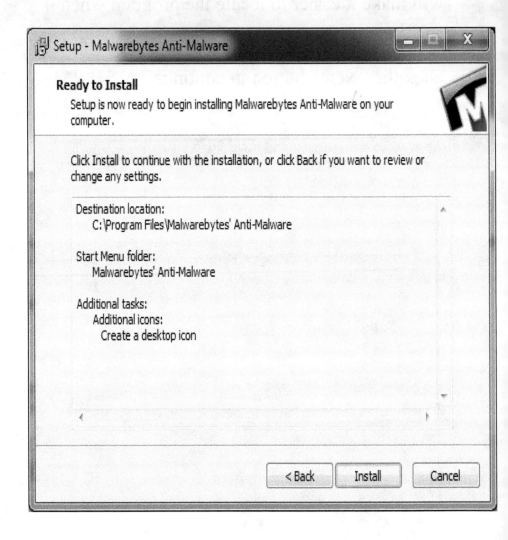

Once the download finishing installing, there will be a prompt to restart your computer. To restart your computer, click the "Finish" button. Tick the "No, I will restart the computer later" button to restart at a later time. Then click the "Finish" button.

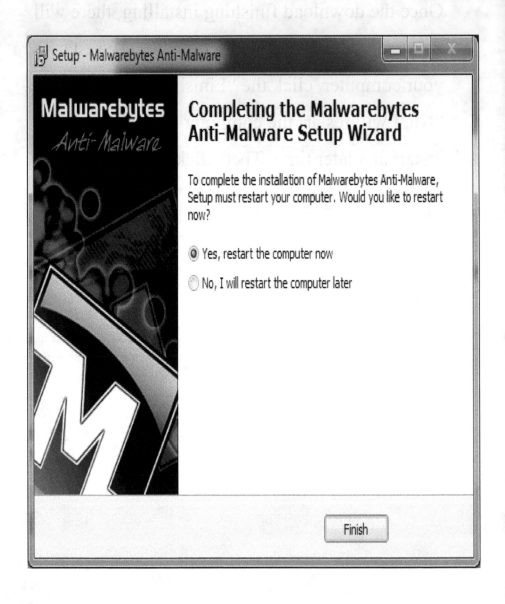

If the "No, I will start the computer later" button
was selected then the installation will not be
complete. The installation will only be complete

upon restarting your computer..

Once the Malwarebytes software is installed locate the icon on your desktop. Double left click to "Open" the program.

Speed Up My Computer

Select by ticking the button next to the full scan and click the "Scan" button. It is recommended to select the full scan if you have not run an Anti-Malware program on your computer. It is a more in depth scan of your computer and does a more thorough scan of your computer.

Full scans can take several hours to complete. The quick scan is faster but may not find all the Malware, Spyware or other malicious programs.

To open the free version, double click on the Malwarebytes icon and follow the prompts. The program, since it is free will need to download updates before running on your computer.
Once the updates are included on your computer it will allow you to select the proper scan for your computer.

It is recommended to perform a scan every day to remove these malicious programs. However, I understand it may not be convenient to perform daily. So I would try to perform a quick scan daily and a full scan once a week.

It is terribly important to find, quarantine, and remove Malware, Spyware and other malicious programs as quickly as possible to prevent damage to your computer.

Thank you for your purchase. I hope you found this manual helpful and easy to follow. Refer back to it anytime you believe you are ready to create more space and defragment your PC.

By following the strategies in this book, your computer should perform at its top performance and be protected from malicious software programs.

If you enjoyed reading this book and it helped you clean up your computer in an easy manor, I like to ask you to consider leaving a review. Simply locate this book in Amazon by clicking the link just below. Scroll down the book page and click on "Write a customer review."

Speed Up My Computer: A Non Techie, Easy to Implement, Step By Step Guide On How to Defrag and Clean Up Your Computer

I would like to thank you for reviewing this book in advance, and I hope you found this book helpful.